Warriors
from the
Secret Place

Dr. Yan G. Venter

Copyright © 2012 Yan Venter Ministries

All rights reserved.

ISBN: 149932099X
ISBN-13: 9781499320992

DEDICATION

I dedicate this book to my wife, Elizabeth.

"Happy is the man who finds a true friend, and far happier is he who finds that true friend in his wife."

CONTENTS

ACKNOWLEDGMENTS	I
1 FROM THE SECRET PLACE	**1**
You're A Somebody	1
2 BRIDLE IT!	**4**
Bridle your tongue	4
Bridle your destiny	7
3 SPEAK TO YOUR MOUNTAIN	**10**
Bad habits	17
Clichés	18
4 MANAGE YOUR WORDS	**21**
The Real Deal	26
5 THE SECRET PLACE	**32**

ACKNOWLEDGMENTS

To our dear friend, Terrie Simmons, for her dedicated work in editing this book. She is absolutely the "kind" I'm writing about. A friendly, quiet and most sincere Christian from *"The Secret Place."*

To my dear wife, Elizabeth, who is always there for me.

To my wonderful Mother In-Law, Miemmie, who is always on time with the next cup of tea...

1 From The Secret Place

You're A Somebody

As I move around in the Church, I find it alarming that the sense of "who we are" in Christ is lacking in so many areas. While the world is expanding in knowledge and yes, "power", it seems that the church is becoming weaker and weaker in a time when we need to provide strong leadership and guidance to a lost and dying world.

We must not forget that we are a city set on a hill. We are supposed to be a light shining in the darkness; but instead of being exactly that, we have become "copy-cats" of Babylon! Instead of being filled with the "dunamis" of God, we have become a weak institution.

Knowing Christ in the power of His resurrection means that we are the bearers of good news. We are world-changers. We have the power to literally change the atmosphere around us!

Demons are supposed to tremble in our presence because of the "One" who dwells in our hearts. We've been given the authority by the Master of the Universe to change the things that need change.

The world around us is literally falling apart! Morals are quickly disappearing; and when anyone talks about morals, they are commonly regarded as being "crazy." However, "alternate lifestyles" are being promoted from the highest levels of society and regarded as necessity!

Our children grow up confused as they observe the diluted influence of the gospel in their homes where moms practice the lies of the Women's Liberation indoctrination, and dads have retracted themselves into the shadows of their "rights" as fathers.

More than 65% of all Christian homes end up in divorce courts at least once in their lifetime, leaving the family ties to deteriorate day after day as peace and tranquility in the home fades away into the mist of yesterday's memory banks. Our society has become sick. The Church is sick. Families are sick; and it seems to become worse and worse every day.

Young people are staying away from church and are following role models that God alone knows where they will lead them. These are role models who themselves are delving deeper and deeper into the occult and drowning in the overwhelming whirlpool of drugs and sex. They are parading onto the platforms across this nation "high" on anything but what is good; and our young people are paying "top dollar" to see them perform. Communication between family members has faded into nothingness, and prayer is something that is only talked about but never practiced.

All of this can and must stop! We can stop it and we should! But it will require a concerted effort to dig your heels in and cry out, "This is the Lord's house! Because we have the Lord as our Maker, MY HOUSE AND I WILL SERVE THE LORD!"

Friend, it must start with YOU! It must start NOW! You must reach a place where you say to yourself, "Enough is enough!" Please carefully consider what this book is about. It is all about your speech! The things that come out of your mouth will determine your future. You are what you tolerate, and what you tolerate is what comes out of your mouth!

You must bring yourself to the place where you connect what you believe to what you speak with your mouth. We are victors in Christ, but this position starts with our confession. Consider what Romans 10:10 says: **"With the heart we believe...but with the mouth confession is made unto salvation!"**

Stop living in regret and guilt for all your failures in yesterday's world. Look at yourself in the mirror and say out loud, *"Yesterday ended at twelve-o-clock last night. Yesterday is gone and there's nothing I can do about it, but today I can start influencing my destiny!"*

In a sense, we are "talking spirits." What I mean by that is the fact that God made us in His image and things changed from the beginning of time when God spoke! You, too, can start identifying with the teaching of the Word by believing that you can bring changes to your own environment by the way you speak.

We always speak! That is the one thing we do so well! The only problem is that we've learned to speak negatively. We've learned to add a "but" to every promise of God. What we need to learn from this book, is that whatever we speak actually determines the pattern of our future.

So, sit back now and enjoy this book; but, when you come to the end, ask God to help you bridle your tongue so that whatever comes out of your mouth, will be confessions of FAITH IN GOD and not FAITH IN FAILURE!

Faith says:
"The Lord is the strength of my life; of whom shall I be afraid?" (Psalm 27:1).
Faith will say about itself everything that the Word says, for faith in God is simply faith in His Person."

2 Bridle It!

James 3:2-4

"For we all stumble in many things (by what we say.) If anyone does not stumble in word, he is a perfect man, able also to bridle the whole body. ₃Indeed, we put bits in horses' mouths that they may obey us, and we turn their whole body. ₄Look also at ships: although they are so large and are driven by fierce winds, they are turned by a very small rudder wherever the pilot desires."

Bridle your tongue

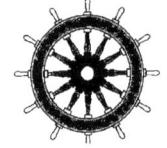

As soon as you turn your focus to this well-read chapter in the Bible, you can remember a whole stack of sermons preached about the "horrors" of gossip. Believe me, gossip is wrong and does a lot more damage than most people realize. But more than gossip is covered in this chapter.

When you consider James 3 within the confines of its text, you will discover that James is saying more in this passage than meets the eye. He is revealing the "secret weapon" that God allows man to carry around with him; namely, the power of speech!

Further in the chapter, James mentions that this

weapon can set the world on fire if used incorrectly. It can destroy people's lives. It can tear a person to pieces. We've seen its destructive power released on churches in the past and it is terrifying! It can severely wound to the point that one may never recover from its devastating blows.

Now, there are certain people who enjoy the power this weapon contains by recklessly throwing words around, seriously wounding others, and watching their victims cringe beneath the severity of the attacks. We must do everything in our power to avoid these evil-minded individuals. Observe the words of the Psalmist in chapter 64, when he says:

"Hear my voice, O God, in my meditation; Preserve my life from fear of the enemy. Hide me from the secret plots of the wicked, from the rebellion of the workers of iniquity, **who sharpen their tongue like a sword**, *and bend their bows to shoot their arrows—*
bitter words, *that they may shoot in secret at the blameless; suddenly they shoot at him and do not fear."*

Who sharpen their tongue like a sword. "Slander has ever been the master weapon of the good man's enemies, and great is the care of the malicious to use it effectively. As warriors grind their swords, to give them an edge, which will cut deep and wound desperately, so do the unscrupulous invent falsehoods, which shall be calculated to inflict pain, to stab the reputation, to kill the honor of the righteous. What is there which an evil tongue will not say? What miseries will it not labor to inflict?"

And bend their bows to shoot their arrows, even bitter words. "Far off they dart their defamations, as archers shoot their poisoned arrows. They studiously and with force prepare their speech as bent bows, and then with cool, deliberate aim, they let fly the shaft which they have dipped in bitterness. To sting, to inflict anguish, to destroy, is their one design. [1]

Those who have felt the edge of a cruel tongue know assuredly that it is sharper than the sword. Slander rouses our indignation by a sense of injustice, and yet we find ourselves helpless to fight with the evil, or to act in our own defense.

We could ward off the strokes of a knife, but we have no shield against a liar's tongue. We do not know who was the father of the falsehood, or where it was born, or where it has gone, or how to follow it, or how to stay its withering influence. We are perplexed, and know not which way to turn. Like the plague of flies in Egypt, it baffles opposition, and few can stand before it.

However, it is not merely the evil who can be involved in this unjust art of warfare, but so can we also from time to time. We also, can inflict great harm by dropping an unguarded word at the wrong time."

We don't intend to cause harm and we wish we never would, but damage can be done. Looking back at my own life, there were times when a harsh word wounded someone; and though my most sincere apologies were offered and the wound healed, the scars were left behind. I hate every moment of it as I look back and remember.

---

[1] C.H. Spurgeon

Bridle your destiny

The essence of James' teaching here however, deals with being in control of your destiny, like sitting on a horse and being in charge of wherever he goes. For this reason he uses the analogy of a bridle:

"We put bits in horses' mouths that they may obey us, and we turn their whole body."

WE, not the horse, decide where he goes. We don't allow any "tricks" from him because we have the reigns in OUR hands. Notice, James is referring to the tongue and the power that it has!

You can decide your future by stating the things you believe. You don't confess your fears, you confess your faith. You don't confess the failures of your past, you confess what you plan to accomplish next.

It doesn't matter how strong the opposing forces are, or the circumstances that stand against your hopes and aspirations. You speak to your situation, as the Bible teaches over and over again. You have been given the authority to do so. Don't let your circumstances speak to you! YOU turn the tables on the situation and YOU speak to the mountain, and YOU let that mountain know what is coming and how things are going to be! Start by acknowledging the situation, then add a "but" to it, by DECLARING how you believe things are going to turn out.

That's probably why James moved from using the horse as an analogy to using a huge ship when he said:

"Look also at ships: although they are so large and are driven by fierce winds, yet they are turned by a very small rudder wherever the pilot desires."

Your situation may seem extremely large, but remember what James says,

"...THOUGH THEY ARE SO LARGE AND DRIVEN BY FIERCE WINDS, THEY ARE TURNED BY A VERY SMALL RUDDER (the words we speak) WHEREVER THE PILOT DESIRES."

It is NOT up to the wind, it is NOT up to the size of the ship, but it all lies in the hand of the pilot "wherever he or she desires." It all hinges on the rudder (our speech!) You can turn things around by the words you speak, either good or bad.

It's appalling to hear a parent say to their youngster, "If you don't want to learn, you'll just be flipping hamburgers someday." While there is nothing wrong with flipping hamburgers, why not steer that ship to a better destiny? Why not say to that child, "Momma knows you're struggling son, but I want you to know that I believe in you. I believe that you will be a success in life, so I will remain on my knees in prayer for you."

Steer that ship away from the rocks, Momma! Speak to that situation as an authorized representative of heaven and declare how <u>you</u> decide the way things will turn out!

Don't confess defeat and run from your situation! <u>Speak</u> to it, and you will discover that it "listens." The Bible says it will, and there's no reason to doubt the Word of God!

Words have power! In the natural realm, words can hurt or heal feelings and attitudes. However, in the spiritual world they contain power that can change your life, direct your future, and help get your life in line with God's Will! Words can literally carry God's power to heal your body, bring financial blessing to your circumstances, and manifest the promises of God's Word in the natural realm to bless you and your family!

Remember the old saying, "Confession brings possession?" Well, that not only applies to the Bible, but to ANYTHING you confess! If you confess the "negative" long enough, you will have it!

2 Cor 4: 7-9; 13(b)
"But we have this treasure in earthen vessels, that the excellence of the power may be of God and not of us. We are hard-pressed on every side, yet not crushed; we are perplexed, but not in despair; persecuted, but not forsaken; struck down, but not destroyed—
I believed and therefore I spoke..."

In metaphysics the higher rules the lower. What we establish in the spiritual realm will manifest in the physical.

Finally, remember we don't have faith in faith; we have faith in God's Word! Our faith is Word-based. Our faith is not faith-based. That's very important to understand, otherwise this teaching will agree with "New Age" principles!

3 Speak To Your Mountain

Mark 11:20-24

*So Jesus answered and said to them, "Have faith in God. For assuredly, I say to you, **whoever says** to this mountain, be removed and be cast into the sea; and does not doubt in his heart, but believes that **those things he says** will be done, he will **have whatever he says**. Therefore I say to you, whatever things you ask when you pray, believe that you receive them, and you will have them."*

Though this scripture has been preached numerous times by many, I still want to take a little time to highlight portions of it, because THIS is the teaching of Jesus. It does not come from Morpheus, the Greek god of dreams; neither does it come from Norman Vincent Peale who is the father of "Positive Thinking." This teaching comes from the One who made all things. Yes, the One who made us in His likeness. (Gen. 1:26)

Jesus teaches us here to "have faith in God," but in fact it should read, "Have the faith OF God," (according to the Vulgate Latin, Syrian, Persian, and Ethiopic versions.) Jesus clearly meant for us to "wake up" to the reality of what God planted in us, namely the authority to act on His behalf. Remember, not on YOUR behalf, or it will plant the erroneous thought in our minds that we are "gods." We act on HIS behalf in matters relating to OUR situation, when He says, "Have the faith of God."

Everything God created was through His Word. He literally spoke things into existence (Rom 4:17). When you face a problem, instead of speaking fear, or doubt or confusion, why not speak "faith?" Speak the God-kind of faith and not the New Age kind or the mere positive-thinking kind, but let the anointing rise up in you and speak like God would speak to that thing!

Three times in this verse, Jesus emphasized the "*saying*" word.

Read it again a few times and let this truth rise up in your spirit. Tell yourself, "I have to watch what I say! Whatever the mountain is, it will not remain in front of me as an obstacle I cannot get over. This mountain will not only hear my voice but it will also hear the voice of God as I speak on His behalf!"

Friend, this is not an erroneous teaching or something new that was created by someone's imagination. This is the teaching of the Son of God and it agrees with everything else we know in Scripture. In the book of Zechariah, we read about the mountain of rubble that remained as a block in front of Zerubbabel. Then the Word of the Lord came to him as follows:

"Not by might nor by power, but by My Spirit, says the Lord of hosts. What are you, O Great Mountain? Before Zerubbabel you will become a plain; and he will bring forth the top stone with shouts of 'Grace, grace to it!'" [2]

---

[2] Zech 4:7

Even though it would be the work of God to bring down this mountain, Zerubbabel had to do his part by speaking to that mountain, "Grace, grace!"

Make up your mind today, that you will not only bridle your tongue to prevent it from going its own way, but bridle your tongue to "go" the way of faith. Let it speak the oracles of God and not the fears of a puny human being who staggers under the shadow of a mountain!

What is a MOUNTAIN in a believer's life? The mountain is any PROBLEM in your life. The mountain is anything that is adverse or contrary to the Word of God for your life. A mountain is anything that is a barrier to completing God's Will for you. A mountain is anything that is slowing down or impeding your progress in the Kingdom of God.

Many believers spend time praying to God about their mountain. They describe the mountain in full detail to God. They inform God of the exact dimensions of the mountain. They cry and moan to God about what a hindrance or impossibility the mountain is in their life. Some people even use the MOUNTAIN as an excuse for nonperformance in their Christian life.

Others make up doctrines and traditions about God, to justify the reason the mountain is still in their life. Still others pray that GOD will speak to the mountain. God will never do what he has commanded you to do! You pray and receive what Jesus has made available to you [Mark 11:24]. It is your responsibility to speak to the mountain in your life!

Praying and fasting will not move a mountain. It deals with unbelief or lack of confidence in God's Word. It crucifies the flesh. Many people get into "natural" unbelief because of what they see, hear, touch, smell, taste or even feel. You must not allow "natural" unbelief to be a counterweight to your faith [Matthew 17:20]. Your unregenerated fallen flesh must not dominate your spirit man!

Prayer concerns your relationship with God through Jesus Christ. Prayer will increase your confidence about your relationship with God. Prayer is the way to receive from God. Fasting food doesn't move God, it moves you. Fasting food takes you out of the natural realm and helps you to be sensitive to the spiritual realm of God. Fasting forces the flesh to submit to the spirit man. God then becomes your total source. You live by the Word of God alone [Matthew 4:3-4].

Fasting retrains or disciplines the body to listen to the spirit man. You tell your body to line up with the Word of God and it obeys you. The spirit man dominates the body or fallen flesh. Prayer does the same thing. Prayer disciplines the flesh to submit to the spirit man. You pray to God, whom you cannot see, hear, taste, smell, or touch [Matthew 6:9, John 20:28]. Prayer trains your flesh to submit to your spirit man. Prayer and fasting are spiritual disciplines.

Prayer and fasting [Matthew 17:21, Mark 9:29] will move you into a more confident [faithful] position to speak to your mountain [Matthew 17:21, Matthew 21:21, Mark 11:23.] Jesus didn't tell us to pray to God about the mountain. He said for us to SPEAK to it. Speak to the mountain in His Name.

Jesus didn't tell us to IGNORE or DENY the mountain or problem. We are not to say, "I don't have a mountain" or *"what problem?"* We are not to practice positive thinking and say over and over, *"I can climb over that mountain, I will go around that mountain; it won't stop me."* A positive attitude is always good. But a positive attitude is not what Jesus said to do with mountains. Jesus said to speak to the mountain or problem and tell it to be moved [Mark 11:23, Matthew 21:21.]

Jesus said that any believer can tell a mountain, **"You be lifted up and thrown into the sea"** [NLT], or **"Go, throw yourself into the sea."** Jesus says, **"If you have faith as a mustard seed, you will say to this mountain, move from here to there, and it will move; and**

nothing will be impossible for you." [Matthew 17:20] A believer [not a doubter] can command the mountain [the problem], "Be moved to some other dimension that I don't inhabit!"

Some of you are praying about things you should be speaking to. You don't need to pray about that fear any more. You need to SAY, "Fear, I command you to leave! I will not allow you to stay in my life!" Instead of begging God to heal you, you need to start saying to that sickness, "Sickness, you have no right in my body! I'm a child of the Most High God! You are not welcome here! And I'm not asking you to leave! I'm not saying 'pretty please' do me a favor! No, I'm COMMANDING you to leave my body!"

If you're going to have mountain-moving faith, you have to SPEAK to your mountains! I've learned, if you don't talk to your mountains, they will talk to you! All through the day...those negative thoughts, "You're never going to get well." "You're never going to get out of debt." "Your business is going to go under." That's your mountain talking to you!

You can sit back and believe those lies or you can rise up and say "Hey, wait a minute! I'm in control here! I'm not going to let this mountain talk to me! Mountain, I'm commanding you to 'Be Removed!' You will not defeat me!"

It's not a coincidence that God chose a mountain to represent our problems. Mountains are big! Mountains seem permanent! It seems like they're going to be there forever! You may be facing a situation right now that looks like it will never change. It looks like you'll never break the addiction. You've had it since high school. It looks like you'll never lose the weight. You've struggled for years. It looks like you'll never accomplish your dreams. There are too many obstacles.

God is saying today, "If you will start SPEAKING to the mountains, you will discover that they are not permanent." That situation that you've dealt with a long time...the sickness, the depression, the addiction...looks like it's not going to change. You've prayed, you've believed, you've quoted scripture. That's all good, but if you're going to see the mountain move, you have to start speaking to it.

When you speak words of faith, something happens in the unseen realm.

Chains are broken. The forces of darkness are defeated. The enemy begins to tremble when you say "Sickness, you have to go!" "Debt, you cannot stay in my life!" "Rebellion, you will not control my child!" "Depression, you will not steal my destiny!"

When you speak, not in your own authority, but in the authority of the Son of the Living God, then all the forces of heaven come to attention. The mighty armies of the unseen Most High God will stand behind you. Let me tell you, no power can stand against our God! No sickness, no addiction, no fear, no legal trouble!

When you speak and do not doubt, the mountain will be removed! It may not happen overnight. You may speak to the mountain and it looks the same month after month. Don't worry about it. In the unseen realm, things are changing in your favor. Remember the account in the Bible where Jesus was walking through a town and He saw a fig tree? He went over to get something to eat, but the tree had no fruit on it. He looked at the tree and proclaimed "You will not produce fruit anymore!"

Notice, Jesus spoke to a tree! People of faith speak to their obstacles. Jesus walked away and it looked like nothing had happened. The tree was just as healthy and green as it was before. I'm sure some of His disciples whispered, "It didn't work. Jesus must have lost His touch 'cause He told it to die but it didn't die!" What they didn't "see" was underneath the ground, in the root system. The moment Jesus spoke, all life was cut off to that tree. When they came back through the town a little later, the disciples stood there in amazement. They saw the tree withered up, totally dead. In the same way, the moment you speak to your mountains, in the unseen realm the forces of heaven go to work. God begins to dispatch angels! He begins to fight your battles!

He begins to release favor! He begins to move the wrong people out of the way; sending healing, sending breakthroughs, sending victory!

You may not see what God's been doing behind the scenes for some time. That mountain may look just as big and permanent and strong as it was before. But if you will stay in faith and keep speaking to the mountain, calling it gone, calling yourself healthy, calling yourself blessed, calling yourself victorious...one day, all of a sudden, you will see that the mountain has been removed!

God will supernaturally do for you what you could not do for yourself.

Jesus didn't pray about the fig tree. He didn't say "Well, I'm believing it's not going to produce any fruit." No, He commanded it not to produce fruit! You have to command sickness to leave your body. You have to command depression to get out of your life. You have to command strife and division to get out of your family.

If you SAY to the mountain "Be removed!" you will have what you say! Here's the key: The mountain responds to your voice! I can speak faith over you all day long. Your friends can build you up with the scriptures. You can put on good music that will encourage and inspire you, and that's all good. But the mountain is not necessarily interested in what I'm saying about you. It's not interested about what your friends are saying to you. It's not even interested in what your parents are praying about you.

Your mountain is paying attention to what YOU'RE saying! It will respond to your voice. When you rise up in faith with your own mouth, saying "Sickness, Addiction, Depression...I'm talking to you! In the name of Jesus, you have to go!" That's when the forces of heaven come to attention!

Bad habits

A bad habit is a negative behavior pattern. It is also defined as follows: "A bad habit or pattern of behavior is something that is repeated so often that it becomes typical of somebody, although he or she may be unaware of it."

Just think about your kids, or even yourself. Can you remember how easy it was for you or them to develop a bad habit? I don't know about your children, but as mine grew up, it was a constant concern to watch for developing bad habits; because the longer a habit is allowed free reign, the more difficult it becomes to break.

Scientists are generally in agreement that it can take as long as twenty eight days to break a habit. But even so, the process must begin with a strong resentment for that habit.

Allowing your mouth to speak negatively is nothing more than a bad habit! We have no reason to doubt God. We have no reason to accept the status quo of a situation when the Word clearly states that we have authority to change it.

Teach yourself to speak "faith" instead of speaking "unbelief." Don't let fear or stress dominate your lifestyle. It offers no promise of improvement. It only brings torment.

Clichés

If there's one thing we are all guilty of, it's the use of clichés! These are words or sayings that have no real meaning. Using a cliché is like the greeter at Wal-Mart saying "Have a nice day!" The fact of the matter is he doesn't really care what kind of day you have!
My wife and I do business with a very "friendly" bank in town. Every time I pull the car up to the window, the friendly clerk asks, "How are you doing today?" One day I decided to take the time to answer her question. For the next few moments I informed her about the things that were happening in our lives. I told her about some of the prayer requests we were dealing with, but while I was "answering" her initial question I could see the frustration building on her face! Some of the other ladies in the bank overheard our conversation and came to the window to see what was happening. It was HILARIOUS! Since that day, she asks only one question when I pull up to the window, and that is "What can I do for you today?"
The same thing is happening in the Church. People shake your hand with "zero" interest and say the usual cliché, "God bless you!" They say it without any meaning. It's empty of substance. It's only a "saying" and nothing more! As "speaking spirits" who have the full authority of God, why not shake the person's hand, look them in the eye and express a meaningful, "God Bless You!" into their lives? We have the authority to change things. We have the authority to make a difference. Friend, we have the authority to steer that "ship" in a direction that pleases God!
The saying, "God Bless You," comes from a Hebrew word that has almost the same meaning in Arabic. The

Hebrew word is "***Berekkah***." Berekkah literally means, "I pronounce God's full and final purpose into your life." That is the ultimate blessing! Releasing God's purpose into a situation is powerful and cannot be diminished by anyone. We are the representatives of heaven. Jesus gave us the keys to the Kingdom to bind and loose, as needed.

Some time ago a pastor-friend of mine informed me with disdain, how a porn shop had opened a few doors away from his storefront church. The pastor expressed his absolute disgust for the situation. But when I asked him what he planned to do about it, he excitedly explained how he stopped outside the business every morning and cursed the place! I smiled as I listened to this frustrated "Man of God" carry-on about this horror that was stealing his joy!

He related that this had been going on for more than two months and firmly stated that he would not relent. "That will not be tolerated!" he said, angrily shaking his finger in the direction of the porn shop. When he was finished, I asked him if his "curses" were working. He confirmed that he had not seen any response yet, but that he would not relent!

Compassionately, I asked if he knew of any scripture where we are encouraged by the Lord to curse anything. Then I reminded him of Romans 12:14, which states ***"Bless them which persecute you: bless, and curse not."***

This humble pastor listened quietly as I explained the full meaning of Berekkah. Then I encouraged him to change his approach. I explained that we have the right to act on behalf of God. "Stop there each morning Pastor, stretch out your hand, and speak a Berekkah toward that place." A few weeks later he called to tell me there was a "For Sale" sign on the door of the porn shop!

The problem with clichés is that they tend to cheapen the things we really want to say. Clichés seem to be clever, and to communicate; but they usually have no substance. They're like the whitewashed tombs Jesus spoke of. They look beautiful on the outside, but inside there's nothing of any value!

In the life of a Christian, clichés can trivialize the most important issues. They can numb the zeal of believers, who may tragically conclude that the sentiments conveyed are no better than the "off-the-cuff" slogans that contain them.

We are an extension of God, and He does not speak to us in clichés. Every word that comes from Him contains life and so must our words. Make your words count, especially when dealing with others. People, as well as the enemy of our souls, can sense when someone really cares. When you speak to that mountain, make the words count and back them up with your faith in God!

4 Manage Your Words

People love to talk. We love to watch "talk" shows. Everybody seems to have something to say. Everyone has something to talk about. Do you know that the average American

Words have POWER

has thirty conversations a day and will spend a fifth of their lives talking? In one year, if all your conversations were written down using your words only, they would fill sixty-six books of eight hundred pages each. On the average in America, a man speaks twenty thousand words a day; and in comparison, a woman speaks thirty thousand.

Some of us are born with a "silver foot" in our mouths. We have the natural ability to say the wrong thing at the wrong time. Our mouths can get us into a lot of trouble!

It is extremely important to make this principle a part of your life, because no matter what your intention is, your words can affect the people around you!

There was a man who lived in New York who was tired of the cold weather, so he decided to go to Florida. His wife was on a business trip at the time, so he called her to let her know what he was doing and to tell her to meet him in Florida. When he arrived he sent her an e-mail to let her know he was there. However, he typed a few letters wrong in the address and instead of going to his wife the e-mail went to a pastor's wife in Iowa whose husband had died the day before.

The little old lady turned on her computer, read the e-mail, screamed and fainted on the spot! Her family and friends who were there came in and found her on the floor. When they saw the message on the screen they understood why she had fainted. The message read: "Dearest Darling, Just wanted you to know I arrived safely. Looking forward to your being with me tomorrow. Signed, Your husband. P.S. -- It sure is hot down here!!!

The book of James speaks more about managing our mouths than anywhere else in the Bible:

"We all stumble in many things. If anyone does not stumble in word, he is a perfect man, able also to bridle the whole body." [3]

James says that if you can control your mouth you'll be perfect. Go ahead and circle the word "perfect." The Greek word for "perfect" does not mean "sinless." It means "mature or healthy." James tells us that to be spiritually mature or spiritually healthy, we must learn to manage our mouths.

Why is it so important to manage your mouth? Look at what Jesus says in Matthew chapter twelve: ***"I tell you that every careless word that people speak, they shall give an accounting for it in the Day of Judgment."*** [4]

Jesus is saying that we will give an account for not only our careless words but for every word we speak; even the careless ones! Words are significant. Words are important. With your words you can build others up and

---

[3] James 1

[4] Matthew 12:36 (NASV)

with your words you can put them down.

Not only were we made in the image of God, but the Bible clearly teaches that He wants us to be like Him in what we say. He has given us that authority, for in Matthew 16:19 He says:

"**And I will give unto thee the keys of the kingdom of heaven: and whatsoever thou shalt bind on earth shall be bound in heaven: and whatsoever thou shalt loose on earth shall be loosed in heaven.**"

This is an incredible truth and must be utilized by the believer.

Isaiah 55:10-11:
"For as the rain and the snow come down from heaven, and do not return there without watering the earth and making it bear and sprout, and furnishing seed to the sower and bread to the eater; So will My word be which goes forth from My mouth; It will not return to Me empty, without accomplishing what I desire, and without succeeding in the matter for which I sent it."

We don't "pretend" to be like God, but as a righteous child of God, you must remember that you are a vessel that contains the precious presence of the Almighty. As I mentioned before, this is not "faith on faith," but faith in God! This principle only works when you really are a child of God. Look what happened in Ephesus in Acts 19:11-16 (NAS):

"God was performing extraordinary miracles by the hands of Paul, so that handkerchiefs or aprons were even carried from his body to the sick, and the diseases left them and the evil spirits went out. But also some of the Jewish exorcists, who went from place to place, attempted to name over those who had the evil spirits the name of the Lord Jesus, saying, 'I adjure you by Jesus whom Paul preaches.' Seven sons of one Sceva, a Jewish chief priest, were doing this. And the evil spirit answered and said to them, 'I recognize Jesus, and I know about Paul, but who are you?' And the man, in whom was the evil spirit, leaped on them and subdued all of them and overpowered them, so that they fled out of that house naked and wounded."

This incident reminds me of the following story,

"An Ass, having put on the lion's skin, amused himself by terrifying all the foolish animals. At last coming upon a Fox he tried to frighten him also, but the Fox no sooner heard the sound of his voice than he exclaimed, 'I might possibly have been frightened myself, if I had not heard your bray.' The moral of the story is often quoted as 'Clothes may disguise a fool, but his words will give him away.'"

One of the most famous questions in the Bible is found in Luke 1:34, where the young Mary asked the Angel, *"How can this be, since I am a virgin?"*

The angel's reply clears it all up for us when we are faced with situations bigger than we think we can handle,

"The Holy Spirit will come upon you, and the power of the Most High will overshadow you..."[5]

"...the Angel drives the nail in deeper when he makes it clear, that *"Nothing shall be impossible with God!"*

A small congregation in the foothills of the Great

---

[5] Verse 37

Smoky Mountains built a new sanctuary on a piece of land willed to them by a church member. Ten days before the new church was to open, the local building inspector informed the pastor that the parking lot was inadequate for the size of the building. Until the church doubled the size of the parking lot they would not be able to use the new sanctuary. Unfortunately, the church with its undersized parking lot had used every inch of their land except for the mountain against which it had been built!

In order to build more parking spaces, they would have to move the mountain out of the backyard. Undaunted, the pastor announced the next Sunday morning that he would meet that evening with all members who had "mountain-moving faith." They would hold a prayer session asking God to remove the mountain from the backyard and somehow provide enough money to have it paved and painted before the scheduled opening dedication service the following week.

At the appointed time, 24 of the congregation's 300 members assembled for prayer. They prayed for nearly three hours. At ten o'clock the pastor said the final "Amen."

Standing up before the prayer group, he decided to take God at His word and SPEAK his faith out aloud: "We'll open next Sunday as scheduled. God has never let us down before, and I believe He will be faithful this time too. I don't know how He's going to accomplish this but I remember the words of the Angels to Mary, when He said, 'Nothing is impossible with God!' We are now going to bed and rest on His promise."

The next morning as he was working in his study, there came a loud knock at his door. When he called "Come in," a rough looking construction foreman appeared, removing his hard-hat as he entered.

"Excuse me, Reverend. I'm from the Acme Construction Company over in the next county. We're building a huge new shopping mall over there and we need some fill dirt. Would you be willing to sell us a chunk of that mountain behind the church? We'll pay you for the dirt we remove and pave all the exposed area free of charge, if we can have it right away. We can't do anything else until we get the dirt in and allow it to settle properly."

The little church was dedicated the next Sunday as originally planned and there were far more members with "mountain-moving faith" on opening Sunday than there had been the previous week!

The Real Deal

This subject cannot be complete without discussing the fact that people not only speak clichés but when they read the Bible, they tend to read "over" the great nuggets that should be delved into and to make it their own.

This problem is huge, because the overall church has a tendency to sit back and merely function on the things that have been "handed down" to them through the years.

> "We are not just one more religion amongst many others. We are the daybreak after midnight, the rainbow after the storm, the table where the Lord invites the hungry to come sit down to feast on the manna that He provides. We are the well of springing water to a soul whose journey brought him through pain and suffering."

We are moving into a very difficult season where the demand on reality is going to be more than ever before. Our nation is in deep trouble. Our churches are in deep trouble and the Lord knows, our families are in serious trouble.

Society has lost interest in the mediocre religious lines that are offered on the unstable foundations of meaningless repetitions. They are literally crying out for the removal of God from the public domain and while it is offensive to you and I, one can almost not blame them, because few churches can back up what they preach because the supernatural remains absent. There remains a brass ceiling above so many and God seems to be a million miles from them! If there is ever a demand for the church to be the CHURCH, then it is at this time. We observe churches going through all sorts of schemes and designs to pull people back after an initial visit, but never to be seen again. Cookie programs and coffee shops are placed as a "carrot" before people who really are not interested in any of that, but they need to make contact with those who know the ways of God and walk in them.

The spirit of religion has replaced the spirit of relationship and it is not strange to walk into most of these "religious clubs" and not feel the awesome presence of God. Clichés and clicks are the order of the day all over this nation and righteous living no longer is the norm. "Christians" live in constant compromise with one foot in the world and the other in the church. Jesus said that the Church is a city on a hill, which means it cannot be overlooked. It means that it is a beacon of hope for the lost and dying who stumble around in a world filled with darkness and destruction. We are not just one more religion amongst a host of others. We are the daybreak after midnight, the rainbow after the storm, the table of the Lord where the hungry are invited to come and feast on the manna He provides. We are the well of springing water to a thirsty soul whose journey has taken him through much pain and suffering.

He also calls us the "salt of the earth." (Matt 5:13) Sodium chloride, or table salt, which can be purchased at the grocery store, is pure. But our modern salt companies did not exist back in the first century. When salt was mined from the quarry or pit, it was never completely pure. Occasionally the salt that was collected was so impure it was not even very salty. When that happened, people would throw it out the front door to line the pathway that led to their homes!

What Jesus was saying was that if we as His followers are going to change the world, we have to be pure salt, we have to be the real deal. Our lives cannot be a mixture of impurities. We have to be uncompromised, pure, and authentic. When Jesus said "You are the salt of the earth," He was saying "Be authentic! Be the real deal!"

An inconsistent lifestyle repels people from the Church. It repels them from coming to know Christ as Savior and Lord. So, how authentic is your walk? Are the people around you drawn to faith because of your life? Do those who cross your path recognize that there is a "difference" in the way you live?

I can't count how many times I've heard people say they know someone who claims to be a Christian, yet that person's life is impure. You truly may be the only Bible that your neighbor may ever read! Are you authentic? Are you the real deal? Or have you let the impurity of the world dilute your saltiness?

- Salt is a preservative
- Salt is an antiseptic
- Salt is seasoning
- Salt is preventative
- Salt is an enemy of decay
- Salt is a foe of impurity
- Salt is an antagonist of rottenness and decay

If the salt loses its savor then there are serious consequences! The key to remaining "salty" is to be authentic; to be real, not attempting to *appear* to be perfect.

In Ancient Greece there were great theatrical events --

stage plays presented in large amphitheaters. There were no microphones to amplify the actor's voices. Likewise there were no cameras to magnify their images, so they invented a system. They created large face masks. These masks caused the actors to look like the characters they portrayed. Megaphones were built into the masks to amplify their voices. When the actors on stage wore the masks, they became someone different than who they really were. The Greeks called this type of actors "*The Hypocrites.*"

There are many people whose lives are nothing more than an act. They play the same roles as the ancient Greeks did. They too, are "*The Hypocrites.*" The promise of the Lord two thousand years ago was that the Church would become a "dynamite entity." He promised that we, the Church, would receive POWER (dunamis) when the Holy Spirit came upon us. (Acts 1:8) Though the word "dynamite" is derived from this root word, and is an appropriate description of the intended character of the Church, at the time of Christ, such a chemical component did not even exist. Therefore, we must dig a little deeper to find the original meaning of this word.

Dunamis is a Greek word for **possibility or capability**. Depending on the context used, it could be translated "potency", "potential", "capacity", "ability", "power", "capability", "strength", "possibility", or "force." It is the root for modern English words such as "dynamic", "dynamite", and "dynamo" (Webster's Dictionary).

When Jesus spoke to the disciples, He said that when the Holy Ghost had come upon them, a supernatural "*enablement*" would occur. Their "*capability*" or lack thereof, would be changed to a "*force*" containing a supernatural "*ability*" to move a mountain or to make a way where there was no way. (Therefore the "dynamite" description is so applicable!)

We are not designed to be some "paralyzed" entity that is incapable of making necessary corrections. Our world is crying for the "manifestation of the sons of God." (Rom. 8:19) Mankind finds itself in a desperate situation for the real Church to "step up to the plate" and declare "We are here to perform the 'impossible' because God has enabled us to become the force that will change the circumstances around us!" Instead, however, the world has fallen into a serious state of decline and decay which is seen not only on the streets, but also in the homes of Christians and churches alike.

It seems as though no one knows what is "wrong" and what is "right" anymore! Christians have become lost in a cloud of heathenism and low morals. Compromise has become the order of the day. Worldliness is the watchword among them, causing the Church and the homes of Christians to become repulsive with the stench of rottenness!

More than 65% of Christian couples end up in divorce court at least once in their lives. Young people have no desire to attend church anymore. In fact, among the top eleven religious nations in the world, the United States ranks lowest in church attendance!

(Refer to the graph on the next page.)

Something must change and it must change NOW! We can delay no longer! Pray today and ask God to help you make the change in YOUR home, in YOUR world! It has to start somewhere, and unless it begins with YOU, it will never happen at all!

Rank	Countries	Amount
# 1	Nigeria:	89%
# 2	Ireland:	84%
# 3	Philippines:	68%
# 4	South Africa:	56%
# 5	Poland:	55%
# 6	Puerto Rico:	52%
# 7	Slovakia:	47%
# 8	Portugal:	47%
# 9	Mexico:	46%
# 10	Italy:	45%
# 11	United States:	44%

5 The Secret Place

As I travel around the world, it is impossible to ignore the pain and suffering in the lives of so many people. Families are broken and splintered. Children are running away from home. Sickness and misery have become commonplace. Churches are filled with confused Christians who commonly suffer from spiritual loneliness, because of an inability to communicate with God themselves.

Satan and his "scallywags" have taken a lead role in the lives of the "pilgrims" to heaven, even though they should never have that kind of authority! Many books are written about the devil, using the term "spiritual warfare" in a way that causes it to take on new meaning for Christians. The fear of the devil is increasing at an alarming rate, even though teaching from the pulpit in most churches makes it clear that "God in us" is greater! The enemy seems to have free reign wherever I go. This is somewhat understandable as the very mention of his name suggests torment. It is a graphic reminder of suffering and pain!

Several years ago during one of my prayer times, I asked the Lord why this situation exists. I reminded the Lord that the "battle arena" in which we must defend ourselves presents an unfair advantage for the enemy. He can see us but we cannot see him. In other words, he can attack and torment us any time he wishes, but we are left vulnerable and seemingly defenseless!

The Lord answered and said the reason for this is because we are too "visible." "Too visible? Lord, you mean we could actually become 'invisible' to the enemy?" For a moment I was speechless as I waited for a revelation from the Lord. When it finally came, God directed me to Psalm 91:1-2, which reads:

"He who dwells in the secret place of the Most High shall abide under the shadow of the Almighty. I will say of the Lord, *'He is* my refuge and my fortress; My God, in Him I will trust.'"

Like most people, I have this psalm flagged in my Bible as one my favorite scriptures. I've read it so many times. I've used it in sermons and quoted it to people in the midst of great storms. In fact, I have it memorized!

Then, in His presence, He directed my attention back to the psalm and explained it in a way that literally left me speechless! A new panoramic view of the truth unfolded before my eyes. Often we glance or read "over" a truth, and it requires revelation from God to enlighten us to see into His deep well of understanding.

Take a moment and read the first two verses of this famous psalm again. "Take my hand" and "walk" with me as I guide you to the same understanding that God gave me:

"He who dwells..." The word "dwell" means: *"to live or stay as a permanent resident."* It's not just a temporary in-out situation; it's a place of habitation. It's where you live, sleep and eat. The sentence starts with "He," which means "the one," or "that person" who dwells there. In other words, it is not automatic. It is a personal choice. Neither does it apply to just any Christian. This is just one of the many verses in the Bible that infers a choice. Many believers claim this psalm for themselves simply because it is in the Bible. However, that is wrong, because it must be a choice that YOU make!

When the Bible says "whosoever", it means anyone,

but here it denotes a specific individual. "That" person, who "dwells" in the secret place, shall abide under the shadow of the Almighty. When I ask people to tell me where the "secret place" is, they invariably tell me it's under the shadow of the Almighty. Not so! THAT PERSON, who LIVES PERMANENTLY in the SECRET PLACE, shall abide under the shadow of the Almighty. When you make your choice to live where God recommends, THEN you will enjoy His protection!

This is not a strange teaching. It coincides with the teaching of Jesus regarding the Kingdom of God in the Parables. You have a choice where you reside - INSIDE the kingdom's walls or OUTSIDE where the thief and robber can attack anytime they choose.

In the old days, each city was surrounded by walls of protection, that featured a wide gate for daytime traffic. After the gates were closed for the night, a small opening, usually about two or three feet square, was available for the "late-comers" to get through. It was called "the eye of the needle." When caravans would arrive after the gates were shut, the only way to get into the city for safety would be through the "narrow gate" or "eye of the needle."

In order for them to enter, they would have to unpack and unload the camels, carry their goods through the narrow opening by hand, and leave the livestock outside. It was not an easy task, so sometimes, they would choose to camp outside the protected area, and wait until morning to enter the main gate. This exposed them to all sorts of dangers; and frequently, they would be robbed and beaten during the night.

The teaching of the Kingdom of God is similar. We have a choice. We can make the effort to "cast down those things that so easily beset us," allowing us to enjoy God's protection; or we can suffer the consequences of staying outside!

"Therefore we also, since we are surrounded by so great a cloud of witnesses, **let us lay aside every weight***, and the sin which so easily ensnares us, and let us run with endurance the race that is set before us."* (Heb. 12:1)

NEXT, we must throw aside weight. What weight? Anything that holds us down and entangles our lives, or our thinking is a weight. When we lay aside unbelief and doubt and take time to observe God's love and ability in every circumstance; acknowledging that it is His accomplishments, not ours, then we can become witnesses and testify of Him!

We must stop saying *"I'll never make it; there's no way; I'm a failure; nobody cares; it's impossible."* Our thinking must be changed. We must concentrate on the times when things worked well, when we were successful. These were the times when there seemed to be no way, no answer and no resources, yet we came through somehow.

Break away today from the habit of confessing defeat. Negative confession is a "weight" that bogs you down. It renders you vulnerable and exposed to the attack of the enemy. Make this your confession today: "I'm moving into the secret place and that's where I'm going to make my permanent abode!"

"He who dwells in the SECRET PLACE..." What is a "secret place?"

It's a hiding place. It's a place where you cannot be found. You are in hiding. It's a place where you cannot be seen nor reached. When you live in the secret place, you dwell under the shadow of the Almighty. If not, you are on your own as "free-bait" for the thief and the robber.

It's a place that needs to be discovered and as I said before, it is not automatic. It takes effort on your behalf to dwell there. I asked God, "You mean I can actually get to a place where the devil cannot see me? Are you saying that

I can really become invisible to the enemy? Can I actually find evidence of this in Scripture, Lord?"

He reminded me of the time when Baby Jesus was born and the enemy tried to get his hands on the helpless baby to kill him. If only he could find the place where Joseph and Mary were hiding, he could kill God's plan; but he could not find them! He tried with everything he had to find the baby, but he could not. Joseph and Mary were in a "secret place!"

Another instance was when the prophet Moses was born. The enemy tried diligently to find the baby since he did not know where he was. We might imagine that as the word came forth from the king to kill every newborn baby boy, that Moses' mother, Jochebed, would have run into the hills to find a cave to hide him in. However, instead she did the unthinkable! She made a woven "chest" of bulrushes, coated it with slime and pitch to make it watertight, and put the child in it. Then she set it afloat on the Nile.

What did God do? He guided that baby down the Nile, right into the "headquarters" of the devil on planet earth, which at that time was undeniably the Egyptian palace! The very ones who were acting out of evil influence to kill the boy, received Moses directly into their home, without the devil knowing that this was the "one" he sought. He could not know, because the boy, Moses, was in a "secret place."

"By faith Moses, when he was born, was hidden three months by his parents, because they saw he was a beautiful child; and <u>they were not afraid of the king's command</u>." (Heb. 11:23)

Now the number one question is, "Where is that secret place, and how do I get there?" The answer to this question is found in Psalm 91:2:

"**I will say** of the Lord, '*He is* my refuge and my fortress; My God, in Him I will trust.'"

That is what brings us into the protection of God, namely, the things we SAY. What does the Psalmist confess? He SAYS, "He is my refuge and my fortress; My God, in Him I will trust!" Faith speaks out! Faith speaks what it believes! Faith makes no room for fear or unbelief. Faith believes and speaks the words God provides.

In closing, let us go back to the beginning of this teaching. What did James tell us in James 3:2-4?

*"For we all stumble in many things. If anyone does not stumble in word, he is a perfect man, able also to **bridle the whole body**. Indeed we put bits in horses' mouths that they may obey us, and we turn their whole body. Look also at ships: although they are so large and are driven by fierce winds, a very small rudder turns them wherever the pilot desires."*

Ask God to help you "bridle" your tongue. Don't speak what you "feel;" speak what you "believe!" Don't confess "fear;" confess "faith" in God's provision! He will never fail you. Remember, it's not merely positive thinking, but it is positively FAITH IN GOD!

ABOUT THE AUTHOR

Yan Venter travels all around the world teaching and preaching the truths about the Kingdom of God.

He holds several degrees, including an earned doctorate from Global University.

The Venter family immigrated to the USA from South Africa in 1985 and now lives in Russellville, AR.

Made in the USA
San Bernardino, CA
11 June 2017